W9-AQO-142

Frog Heaven

Ecology of a Vernal Pool

Doug Wechsler
Photographs by the Author

BOYDS MILLS PRESS

HONESDALE, PENNSYLVANIA

Central Islip Public Library
33 Hawthorne Avenue
Central Islip, NY 11722-2498

235 8154

ACKNOWLEDGMENTS

I would like to thank people who provided me with information about vernal pools and their inhabitants, including Ned Gilmore of The Academy of Natural Sciences, Leo Kenney of The Vernal Pool Association, Bill McAvoy of the Delaware Natural Heritage Program, and Jim Dobson of Blackbird State Forest. Dr. Betsy Colburn of Harvard Forest reviewed the manuscript and offered many helpful comments. I am also grateful to Betty Tatham, Ned Gilmore, Charlie McCooe, and my wife, Debbie Carr, for reading and commenting on the manuscript. Finally, thank you to the many people who accompanied me while studying this pond, including Katrina Macht and her students.

—D. W.

Text and photographs copyright © 2006 by Doug Wechsler
All rights reserved

Boyds Mills Press, Inc.
A Highlights Company
815 Church Street
Honesdale, Pennsylvania 18431
Printed in China

Library of Congress Cataloging-in-Publication Data

Wechsler, Doug.
  Frog heaven : ecology of a vernal pool / by Doug Wechsler ; photographs by the author.— 1st ed.
    p. cm.
  Includes bibliographical references.
  ISBN-13: 978-1-59078-253-8 (hardcover : alk. paper)
  1. Vernal pool ecology. I. Title.

  QH541.5.P63W43 2006
  577.63'6—dc22

    2005037562

First edition, 2006
The text of this book is set in 12-point Palatino.

Visit our Web site at www.boydsmillspress.com

10 9 8 7 6 5 4 3 2 1

For my uncommonly lovely wife, Debbie, who also loves nature

Introduction

No Fishing!

IMAGINE A POND WHERE YOU COULD FISH ALL DAY and never even catch a minnow; where you could walk across and sometimes not even get your feet wet; and where the calls of frogs on a warm spring night will pound your eardrums. Welcome to frog heaven—a vernal pool.

You are about to spend a year in and around a large vernal pool in the woods of Delaware. A vernal pool is a seasonal pond. The pool fills and dries out over the course of the year. Though it is not always full of water, it is full of life.

A vernal pool is a special kind of pond. Three things make a pond a vernal pool. First, it dries out at some time in most years. Second, no permanent stream flows into or out of it. And third, it has no fish.

You might think that drying up would harm the pond life. Actually, it helps the vernal-pool life because fish and some other predators that would eat frogs and other animals cannot survive in a dried-up pond. The pool's ecology (the relationship between and among its plants, animals, and environment) is tied to this cycle of filling and drying. As you will see, the same thing that makes this pond a lousy place for fish makes it a great place for frogs and many other animals to live.

Vernal pools go by many names. One local name is whale wallow. *This comes from the unrealistic idea that stranded whales formed the pools by thrashing around. Large vernal pools on the Delmarva Peninsula are called Delmarva Bays. The Delmarva Peninsula is made up of parts of Delaware, Maryland, and Virginia. Delmarva Bays are large, as vernal pools go.*

5

Autumn: smartweed, grasses, and beggar-ticks (the plant in front with the dark balls of seeds on top) cover the dry pool bottom.

Chapter 1

Marbled salamander

Autumn Migrations

AUTUMN LEAVES ARE TURNING in central Delaware. As you look around the vernal pool, you see purple, red, yellow, green, and brown. The pond is dry. Not even a puddle of water remains. The bed of mud that was once the bottom of the pool is now a field of grasses, smartweed, and yellow-flowered beggar-ticks.

Winter will be here soon. Is this the time to begin a story about some ponds? Is this really heaven for frogs? Yes. Yes. You will soon learn why.

Autumn is the end of the annual cycle for many plants and animals. The countdown to winter has started. Some forest birds are migrating far to the south. Plants must finish producing their seeds. Many of the seeds will lie dormant in the mud until the pond fills and dries again. As autumn ends, the dry pond bed is covered with the leaves of deciduous trees—trees that lose their leaves for the winter.

Though many animals start their life cycles in spring, marbled salamanders are just beginning theirs in autumn. October rains send marbled salamanders migrating from the woods to the dry ponds. While other mole salamanders lay their eggs in water, marbled salamanders lay them on land. The female lays about one hundred eggs beneath the leaves, under a log, or in a hollow within the dry vernal pool. She stays with the eggs to protect them, sometimes for two months or more. Autumn breeding gives marbled salamanders a jump on the other ten species of amphibians that breed in the pool.

Autumn rains bring new life to the vernal pool.

Marbled salamanders come out of the ground to lay eggs beneath the leaves of the dry pool.

A common spreadwing damselfly rests on a twig above the pool.

Marbled salamanders are not the only creatures getting started in fall. A small dragonfly, called a blue-faced meadowhawk, lays her eggs on the dry pond bed. Adult caddisflies also migrate to breed in the dry pool from tree holes where they have spent the summer.

As autumn wears on and the sun rises later and later, the plants go to seed and die. The pond looks lifeless, but a new beginning is near.

Not-So-Mysterious Force

In the dry pond bed, deep beneath a hollow log, lies a marbled salamander curled around her eggs. This chunky, 4-inch-long black-and-white amphibian is waiting for something.

Among the dead leaves on the moist ground are microscopic eggs. They are eggs of fairy shrimp, caddisflies, and dragonflies. All lie dormant. All are waiting for the mystery force.

Isopods are ¹/₂-inch- (12-millimeter-) long crustaceans with seven pairs of legs. These aquatic relatives of sow bugs crawl on the pond bottom, eating and shredding dead plants and animals. This recycles food for other creatures in the pond.

Deep beneath the surface in the dark, cool ground lies the force that will soon end the waiting. As late autumn rains continue, it creeps up through the soil. Slowly this force reaches the salamander and her eggs. It surrounds the eggs of the caddisflies. It brings new life and starts new cycles.

What is the mystery force? It is water. Water is the main ingredient of life.

Water acts as a natural stopwatch. It starts and stops natural cycles. Here at the vernal pool, water and the sun keep time for the natural world.

Water allows eggs of the salamanders, insects, fairy shrimp, and many other tiny creatures to hatch. It brings other creatures such as snails and shrimplike animals called scuds out of the soil on the bottom of the pond where they have been dormant. When the water covers her eggs, the mother salamander returns to the woods.

The pond rises because of the autumn rain and the cooler weather. How does weather change the depth of water in the pond? In summer, the warm sun evaporates water from the pond and the soil into the air. The sun's energy also fuels the growth of trees. Trees suck water out of the ground to grow. They suck up more water than they need, and much of it is lost through the leaves. In the fall, when the temperature is cooler, there is not so much evaporation, so rainwater stays in the ground. Trees stop growing and lose their leaves, so water they would use stays in the ground instead of going into the air. As the groundwater rises, it fills the pond and the pond's life is reborn.

Leaves and fruits as well as flowers of the sweet-gum tree will later become food for life in the vernal pool.

Winter: beneath the ice, many small creatures are active.

Chapter 2

Tiger salamanders come into the ponds in winter to breed.

Winter: Not All Is Frozen

THE FOREST IS QUIET AROUND THE POOL. A flock of sparrows feeds on seeds at the edge of the pond. Deer leave their tracks in the snow. Where are the frogs, salamanders, and insects?

The marbled-salamander eggs are hatching beneath the water. The 1/2-inch (12-millimeter) larvae will feed on tiny animals about the size of this small letter o. These include daphnia, or water fleas; copepods; and seed shrimp, all of which spent the summer as eggs waiting for the pool to fill with water. The salamanders and their prey will stay active beneath the ice.

The salamanders that breed in the pond live most of their lives underground. The ground in winter freezes only near the surface. Salamanders can easily avoid freezing by staying deep below this frozen layer of soil in shrew tunnels and spaces between tree roots. There they wait quietly for warmer weather.

Bullfrogs move to permanent ponds for the winter if the vernal pool is dry in fall.

Wood frogs, treefrogs, and chorus frogs meet winter head on. They simply dig down into the leaves. As the weather gets cold, a wood frog's liver produces a great deal of sugar. When the temperature drops below 32°F (0°C), the frog starts to freeze, too. Sugar from its liver goes into its blood and inside the body's cells, acting as an antifreeze. Only parts of the body between the cells freeze. If snow covers the "frogsicle's" leafy hiding place, so much the better. Snow forms a blanket between the ground and the cold air. It keeps the ground temperature near the freezing point, even when the air is much colder. As long as the frog does not get colder than 17°F (-7°C), it will survive being frozen.

Other frogs moved away from the pool when it dried out at the end of summer. Bullfrogs and green frogs moved to nearby farm ponds and streams. They avoid freezing by hiding in the muck of these ponds or running streams.

Bullfrogs are the largest frogs in North America. They eat just about any animal smaller than themselves, including other bullfrogs. The call of the bullfrog is unmistakable—a deep, slow "jug-o-rum."

Bullfrogs cannot breed in vernal pools because their tadpoles take a long time to develop. The tadpoles need at least a year to grow into frogs, but the pond will be dry before that. Some bullfrogs come to vernal pools to feed, but drying pools keep their numbers in check.

In the cold, rising water of the pond, life is bustling. The water is filled with fairy shrimp, water beetles and their larvae, and caddisflies. Caddisfly larvae crawl around on the bottom beneath the ice. They look something like caterpillars, but they are hard to see. This is because they hide inside tubes made with bits of leaves or sticks from the bottom of the pond. These homes are the perfect moving camouflage. Each species of caddisfly makes its own kind of tube, which it carries around on its body. Like caterpillars, the larvae grow, then pupate. After a resting period, they fly from the pond looking like small moths and will return later to lay their eggs in the dry pool bottom or in the water.

Caddisflies perform an important service for the pond community. They shred and eat dead leaves that have already been partly decomposed by bacteria and fungi. Caddisflies, isopods, and midge larvae turn the dead leaves into a kind of food that other animals can use. They are freeing the energy that the leaves captured in the sun and moving it on its way through the food web. Bacteria, tadpoles, and

Caddisfly larvae help turn leaves into food for other animals by chewing and shredding the leaves.

isopods eat the bits of leftover leaves and the caddisfly droppings.

Water beetles play an important role as predators in the ecology of vernal pools. Some of the many species fly away from the pool when it dries up to spend the winter in permanent ponds, then return in spring. Others spend the dry period beneath the leaves of the pond bottom and become active again when the pool fills. Some stay active through the winter.

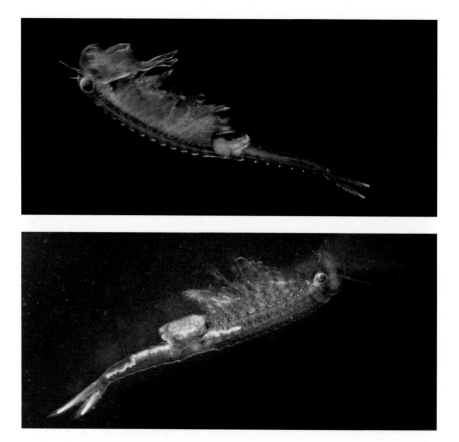

Fairy shrimp live only in vernal pools. The male, above, has large antennae in front that he uses to grasp the female. The female, below, has a brood sac behind her legs to hold eggs.

Fairy shrimp are crustaceans. Like lobsters, shrimp, crabs, and all other crustaceans, they have tough outer exoskeletons and jointed legs. Fairy shrimp swim upside down, rowing with eleven pairs of legs. The movement of their legs sweeps tiny creatures, bacteria, algae, and fine debris toward their mouths. Much of the debris comes from leaves shredded by caddisfly larvae and then further broken down by other small creatures. As the season moves on, these alien-looking fairy shrimp grow to 1/2 inch (12 millimeters) or more. Their bodies are translucent—light shines right through them. You can clearly see the dozens of eggs that the females carry inside a pouch.

Eggs of fairy shrimp must dry and get wet again before they can hatch. Not all eggs will hatch the following year when the pool fills again. Some will stay dormant in the mud on the bottom of the pond for years. Only some hatch each year. The same is true for the eggs of some other crustaceans such as copepods, seed shrimp, and daphnia, or water fleas. Even if all of the fairy shrimp are wiped out in a bad year because of drought or a flood that brings fish into the pond, they will survive since extra eggs are waiting to hatch.

Fairy shrimp are vernal pool obligates. That means they can live only in vernal pools or other seasonal wetlands. Like many amphibians, they are easy prey for fish. Since vernal pools do not have fish, they make good homes for fairy shrimp. Some kinds of fairy shrimp have become endangered because many of the pools they live in have been destroyed.

Tigers on the Move

A brief break in the winter weather, even in the middle of January, is enough to set the tiger salamanders in motion. From their underground homes in the surrounding woodlands, they come to the surface and enter the ponds on a rainy night. Tigers are the largest of the vernal-pool salamanders, usually about 8 inches (20 centimeters) long. They will spend the next few weeks in the pond. There they will lay their eggs. The eggs hatch at the end of winter. The marbled salamanders that got a head start on growth in the fall will eat some of the tiger-salamander larvae.

As spring draws near, life in the pool is busy beneath the surface. In the woods around the pool, all is quiet except for a few birds warming up their voices for spring. With a couple of warm days, all will change.

A tiny male spring peeper calls to attract a mate.

Chapter 3

A male chorus frog sings from the surface of the water.

Spring Symphonies

Quacking, piping, and creaking sounds fill the air. Who is making all the racket? Frogs singing their love songs, signaling the change from winter to spring. Suddenly in early March, the Delaware woods have come alive. Following the sound, you soon find yourself at the edge of a pond. The calls of wood frogs, spring peepers, and chorus frogs almost make your ears ring.

The quacking calls come from wood frogs. Wood frogs look as if they are wearing robber's masks and quack like ducks. These 1½- to 2½-inch (4- to 6-centimeter) frogs come in tan, brown, and rust, matching the colors of dead leaves lying on the bottom of the pond. To our ears, the noisy calls of wood frogs announce, "Spring is here." To others of their own kind, the quacking says, "Come and mate!"

Although they are in a huge pool, wood frogs mate and lay eggs in one tiny part of the pool.

Explosive Breeders Don't Pop

Wood frogs are explosive breeders. This does not mean that they pop while laying eggs. An explosive breeder breeds in a flash of time. Within a day or so of the first warm weather, nearly all of the wood frogs are hopping to the pond. They have spent a lazy winter hibernating under leaves or logs. Now they seem to be in a terrible hurry. Sugar in their blood that had protected them from freezing is now their fuel. They will not eat until they are done breeding.

The male wood frogs choose one or two choice spots in the pond to gather and blurt out their spring chorus. The larger females all show up within a day or two. After mating and laying eggs, the females leave the pond. Within two days, nearly all the eggs are laid. The males keep singing for another week or so, hoping another female will show up.

A female wood frog lays eggs underwater while the male fertilizes them.

Rapid breeding in early spring has advantages for the wood frogs. It is still too cold for the water snakes, bullfrogs, and other predators that would eat them. Getting a head start on most salamander larvae means the tadpoles will be too big to be eaten. Most critically, the tadpoles will have time to develop into small wood frogs before the pool dries up. After

Wood frogs lay up to one thousand eggs in a jelly-like mass. Water will make the jelly expand to protect the black-and-white eggs.

breeding, wood frogs return quickly to their home in the woods, where they can feed and find shelter.

Within two weeks the wood frogs have come and gone. Hundreds of jelly-like clusters with small black dots are all that remain. Each egg cluster contains about a thousand eggs. Together, the many clusters of eggs cover an area about the size of a truck tire. A quarter million eggs will be hatching in a couple of weeks.

The forest is the home of the wood frog. The vernal pool is only their breeding ground and nursery. When they hop off into the woods, the quacking stops, but the piping of spring peepers and creaking of chorus frogs continue for a few more weeks. Then they, too, will leave the water. Though we think of ponds as the home of frogs, most species of frogs spend much of their lives away from water.

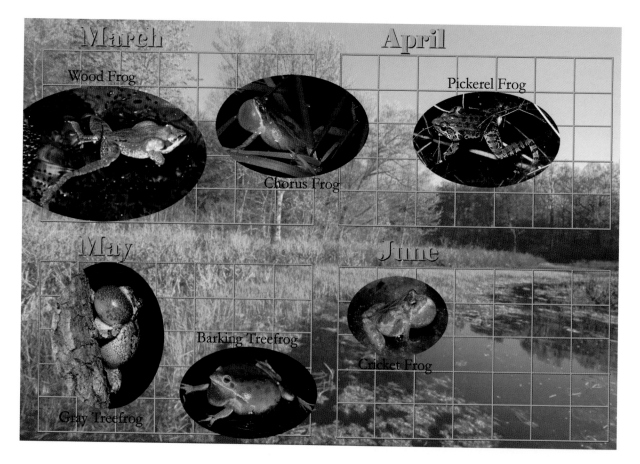

You can tell what part of spring it is by listening to the calls of frogs.

You can measure the progress of spring by the voices of frogs. As we saw, the first warm weather at the end of winter brings the "quacks" of wood frogs. The loud piping whistles of tiny spring peepers will soon follow, along with the creaking love songs of chorus frogs. Both of these will be singing for another month or more. The "snoring" of pickerel frogs means April has come. A chorus of gray treefrog trills heralds May, and the whooping of the barking treefrog and the clicking of the northern chorus frog mean summer is about a month away. Unlike the wood frogs, these other frogs spread out their breeding seasons. Each will call for several weeks.

Spotted salamanders arrive in the vernal pool with the first warm spring rains.

Spotting Spotted Salamanders

Spotted salamanders usually move from the woods to the ponds as the wood frogs are leaving. These large, black terrestrial salamanders sport cheery yellow polka dots. Because of their good looks and the fact that they breed in these ponds, they have become a symbol of the vernal pool. Spotted salamanders are also explosive breeders. If the weather is just right, a warm rainy night in March will bring hundreds of spotted salamanders out of the ground to migrate to the pools to breed. Salamander watchers call this "big night."

A closeup view of spotted salamanders developing inside the eggs

After a big night, spotted salamanders will spend only about a week in the water. In years when rains stop or it suddenly gets cold again, the salamanders may straggle to the pool over the course of several weeks. During this time they breed, and each female lays about one hundred eggs. The fist-sized clusters of jelly-covered eggs can be found on underwater sticks throughout the pond. Unlike wood-frog eggs, the salamander eggs will take a month or more to hatch.

Unfortunately, few people see spotted salamanders because they are nocturnal, or active at night, and spend most of their time in burrows of shrews, voles, and moles and other natural holes underground in the woods. Because of their underground lifestyle, spotted salamanders and their relatives are called mole salamanders. Most people do not

Central Islip Public Library
33 Hawthorne Avenue
Central Islip, NY 11722-2498

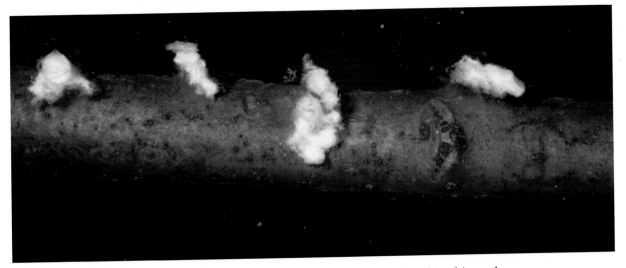

Spermatophores like these are a sure sign that spotted salamanders breed in this pool.

During the breeding season, when spotted salamanders visit vernal pools, they can usually be seen only at night. During the day, you can tell that they have arrived by the spermatophores that the males leave behind. Spermatophores are white, jelly-like packets that males deposit on sticks or leaves. The female salamander picks up the spermatophores with her cloaca, the opening where eggs and waste leave the body. Then her eggs are fertilized inside her body.

even know that these salamanders exist. When they are discovered, their smiley-looking mouths and bright yellow spots win people over. If more people were familiar with spotted salamanders, they would probably take better care of the pools instead of filling them with dirt to dry them up.

A Wealth of Amphibians

Nine species of frogs and five species of salamanders breed in this vernal pool! That may be a record number of amphibians breeding in one pond for any place this far north around the world.

What makes this place ideal for amphibians? First of all, there are no fish. This pool is not connected to any stream, so no fish can enter. It also dries out most years, so no fish can survive.

Fish are mortal enemies of wood frogs, spotted salamanders, and many other amphibians. Small fish gobble down amphibian eggs and larvae. Large fish, like bass, also gulp down adult frogs and salamanders whole.

Another reason vernal pools are great for amphibians is that they are shallow. Even at its deepest point in the wettest

A four-toed salamander spends most of its life in the woods but breeds in the vernal pool.

year, the water in this pond is only a few feet deep. Shallow water warms up quickly as spring moves along. Amphibians, and the animals they eat, grow faster when the water is warm.

The alternate drying and filling of the pools helps to decay the dead leaves. As the leaves break down, they provide a lot of nutritious food for amphibians and their prey.

Some amphibians, such as wood frogs and mole salamanders, breed only in vernal pools and similar wetlands. Like fairy shrimp, they are obligate vernal pool species. If we lose these pools or the woods around them, the obligate species will also disappear.

What Fuels the Pond?

We run our cars on gasoline and our toasters on electricity. We fuel our bodies with food. All of this energy originally came from the sun. The same is true for vernal pools.

The sun is one big ball of energy. Even though it is 93 million miles (150,000,000 kilometers) away, it gives off enough heat and light to fuel life in the vernal pool (and the rest of the earth). Plants use the energy of the sun to make their own food and to grow leaves. When leaves die, the warmth of the sun allows bacteria and fungi to decompose them. Caddisfly larvae that eat and shred decomposing leaves are using the energy of the sun in the leaf as fuel. The tadpoles that eat shredded leaves and their decomposers use energy stored in the plants and decomposers that first came from the sun. The

A wood-frog tadpole munches the slime on a decomposing leaf.

snake that eats the tadpole gets its energy from the tadpole, which got its energy from the leaves, which got energy from the sun. All the energy that drives the life in the pond came at one time from the sun.

The sun is also keeper of the clock. When the sun rises late and sets early, it is a cue for trees and bushes to drop their leaves. When days grow longer at the end of winter, plants open their buds and birds start to sing. Though water fills the pond, starting an annual cycle, it is the sun that dries it out, bringing the cycle to a close.

Who Eats Whom?

Fueled by sunlight, leaves grow on forest trees. The leaves fall in autumn into the dry pool. As the pool fills, bacteria and fungi grow as a film on the leaves and decompose them. Insects and worms feed on the decomposing bits of leaf and on the film. Wood-frog tadpoles snarf up both the film of decomposers and small animals in the film. Herons eat those tadpoles. This is a food chain. There are many food chains in

A leopard frog tadpole falls prey to a green heron.

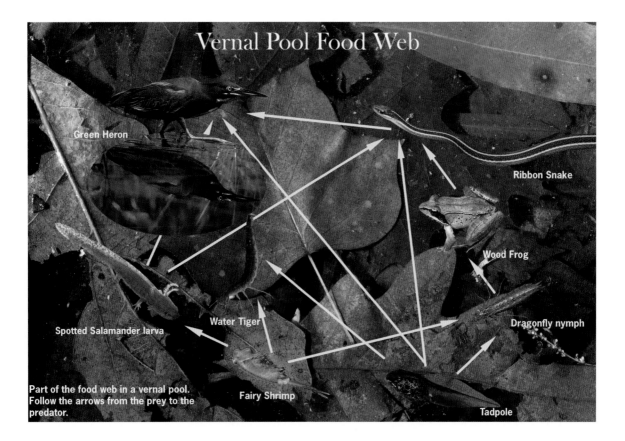

Vernal Pool Food Web

Green Heron

Ribbon Snake

Wood Frog

Spotted Salamander larva

Water Tiger

Dragonfly nymph

Fairy Shrimp

Tadpole

Part of the food web in a vernal pool. Follow the arrows from the prey to the predator.

the ponds. For example, the same tadpoles could be eaten by a water beetle larva called a water tiger, which could be eaten by a dragonfly larva, which could be gobbled up by a red-winged blackbird after the larva comes out of the pool to change into an adult. Food chains are connected to other food chains. Together they form a food web. Try to create your own food web. As you read this book, draw a chart of the plants and animals in a vernal pool. When you finish the chart, draw lines connecting the predators and their prey. Your drawing should look like a spider web.

Beneath the Surface

While choruses are filling the air with strange noise, plenty is happening underwater. In May, wood-frog tadpoles that hatched in March are sprouting tiny legs near the base of

The ribbon snake is a slender species of garter snake that spends most of its time in and near water. The ribbon snake dines on frogs and tadpoles in vernal pools. It is one of the first active snakes in spring.

The middle of the pool in spring, just before the buttonbush leafs out

their tails. Soon their arms will pop out their sides, and in a few more days, a small frog will be hopping from the pond to live its life in the woods. At about the same time, young marbled salamanders will lose their bushy gills and also metamorphose, becoming adults. *Metamorphosis* is the change in an animal from one life stage to another. During a big rain in early June, salamanders will crawl out from the pond and enter their woodland homes.

Wood frogs are the first amphibians in the pool to metamorphose, or change to adult form.

In the pond, tadpoles and salamander larvae of many kinds and sizes continue to grow. As summer approaches, they face a growing number of enemies, including water beetles, water bugs, bullfrogs, water snakes, and ribbon snakes. Small tadpoles also fall prey to hungry salamander larvae.

Southern leopard frogs seem equally at home on land and in the water. They range from green to brown but can always be recognized by their oval, dark spots. They usually lay their eggs in spring, but a few may breed at any time until October. Leopard frogs do very well in large vernal pools that are not completely shaded by the forest. They breed in many other types of wetlands but spend much of their adult lives in meadows and other open areas.

As the pool dries in summer, young amphibians, like these leopard frogs, must metamorphose or die.

Chapter 4

A barking treefrog tadpole

Summer: Time to Wrap Things Up

SUMMER STARTS A RACE AGAINST TIME. The heat of the sun dries the landscape. Since much of the water in the pond comes from the ground, the pond gets shallower. What will happen to the community of animals thriving in the water?

Danger! Shrinking Pool

As a vernal pool gets shallower, the sun warms the water faster. In the warm water, salamander larvae and tadpoles grow faster. It is a dangerous time for life in the pool. The pool is shrinking. Soon it is only a puddle—a puddle swarming with life. You might call it a tadpole soup. The soup is spiced with water beetles, water scorpions, dragonfly larvae, and many other creatures. A green heron is drawn to this

Dragonfly nymph and smaller damselfly nymph

The nymph of a large dragonfly

soup. It spies the movement of the tadpoles in the murky, dark water and gobbles them down with ease. With their sensitive fingers, raccoons also have an easy time hunting amphibians at night. The young amphibians have no place to hide in the tiny pool.

Some tadpoles and salamander larvae change into adults just in time. During metamorphosis, a tadpole changes rapidly into a very different animal. The new animal has a large jaw, four legs, no tail, and big eyes. Inside it develops a pair of lungs, a larger stomach, and a shorter intestine. We know this animal as a frog, of course.

Salamander larvae look much like adults, but they change as well. Before they move onto land, salamanders lose their tail fin and grow stronger legs and a larger mouth. They lose their bushy gills and develop lungs to breathe air.

Tadpoles and salamander larvae that do not change in time die as the last puddle dries up. The dead tadpoles lie in what was once the deepest part of this pool. The rotting tadpoles attract scavengers—animals that eat dead animals. Flies are the most common scavengers, but even huge turkey vultures may glide down for a gross meal. As tadpoles decay, butterflies probe in the mud nearby to get salts that came from the tadpole bodies. What the maggots, vultures, and butterflies do not eat will become fertilizer for the plants that will soon grow on the dried pond bed. In nature almost everything is recycled.

If the pool dries early, tadpoles will die. Fly larvae, called maggots, eat and recycle the tadpoles.

You might think that drying would destroy the pond. The special thing about vernal pools is that drying actually keeps them healthy. A drying pond will kill any fish that have found their way into the pool. If fish could survive in the pond, they would eat the eggs and larvae of salamanders and frogs. Hungry bullfrogs must leave when the water is gone. Bullfrogs have a big appetite and devour lots of other frogs. Some large dragonflies, whose nymphs prey on tadpoles and salamander larvae, take more than a year to complete their life cycle. They are eliminated when the pool dries. Other predators must also leave or die. This includes water snakes, turtles, giant water bugs, and water beetles. When the pond

A red-spotted purple butterfly sips up salts from the bodies of dead tadpoles.

finally fills up again in late autumn, it will take a while for these predators to find their way back. Meantime, the tadpoles and young salamanders will have a head start.

With the drying of the pond, you might think that all the frogs would leave. Some do. Adult bullfrogs and green frogs hop over to nearby farm ponds and streams that have water year-round. Leopard frogs, cricket frogs, and some of the young bullfrogs and green frogs stay around. They feed on the many insects and spiders that populate the dried-up pond.

Tracks of a raccoon that visited the drying pool at night to feed on tadpoles

Busy Bush

In midsummer, about the time the pond usually starts to dry out, buttonbush comes into bloom. This is the only bush growing in the center of the pond. Many inch-wide creamy balls of flowers cover the bush.

At first glance, buttonbush is not so remarkable. But look at how many ways it connects to the other life in the pond. During a typical early summer, the bottom 2 1/2 feet (75 centimeters) of the bush is underwater. The jungle of

The Fowler's toad did not breed in this pool, but it visited after the pool dried up to feed on insects.

On the dried edge of the pool, meadow beauty blooms in summer.

underwater stems has plenty of hiding places for frogs trying to escape from turtles. Its tangle of underwater twigs is a good place for chorus frogs and spotted salamanders to lay their eggs.

Dragonfly and damselfly larvae hunt smaller insects and tadpoles from the underwater buttonbush twigs. Later in the season, the larvae will crawl up a stem at night and leave the water. There they will hang helplessly from a twig higher up on the buttonbush. Slowly they break out of their exoskeletons while their wings expand. The exoskeletons are the hardened outer coverings of insects that give shape to their bodies. In the early morning, red-winged blackbirds hunt these dragonflies and damselflies before they can fly. Once the dragonflies can take to the air, they use the tops of the buttonbushes as lookout posts. They warm themselves in the sun, keeping their eyes out for prey and for other dragonflies.

Two red-winged blackbirds build their cup-shaped nest in the crown of a buttonbush a few inches above the pond. There over the water, the speckled eggs and chicks are safer from foxes, raccoons, and mice that would have to swim to get them. The redwings also feed their growing young the many aquatic insects emerging from the pond. The crowns of

Just out of its nest in a buttonbush, a fledgling red-winged blackbird stretches its wing. Its father brings damselflies for breakfast (right).

A spangled skimmer dragonfly rests on a buttonbush twig.

the buttonbushes also hold basking water snakes in early spring. As the leaves come out in spring, the hairy caterpillars of tiger moths and tussock moths eat the greenery.

In July, the cream-colored ball-shaped flower clusters bloom. Butterflies from far and wide flutter in to sip the buttonbush's sweet nectar. At the same time, they carry the dusty pollen from bush to bush and pollinate the flowers.

When autumn comes, spiders lay their silk-covered eggs

A monarch drinks nectar from a buttonbush bloom (left). A barking treefrog sits scrunched up during the day to keep from drying out.

high on the crowns of the buttonbushes, where they will stay dry until they hatch next spring. Soon the drying leaves will fall. Later, when the pond fills, the leaves will feed caddisfly larvae, isopods, and aquatic worms.

These are just a few ways that the buttonbush is important to life in this vernal pool. Like the buttonbush, every plant and animal in the pool is connected to the lives of other plants and animals. Each is tied to the pool in many ways.

As summer ends, the last patches of mud in the center of the pond are growing a new green carpet of beggar-ticks, grasses, and other plants. An occasional leopard frog can be seen hopping through the plants, but other frogs are gone or hiding. Who would dream that this is heaven for frogs?

A marbled orb weaver comes out of its hideaway in a buttonbush leaf (top). A white-marked tussock-moth caterpillar lives and feeds on buttonbush.

In autumn, buttonbush leaves will drop into the dry pool and become part of the food web of the vernal pool.

Vernal pools are easily damaged and need protection.

Chapter 5

A young red-spotted newt

Vernal Pools—Don't Let Them Dry Up Forever

IT TOOK THOUSANDS OF YEARS FOR THIS VERNAL POOL to become what it is today. It took millions of years for the vernal-pool animals and plants to blend their cycles together. It takes a bulldozer a few minutes to destroy a pool forever.

Fortunately, this frog heaven is protected by the state of Delaware. Many other pools nearby are not on state land and have not been so fortunate. Farmers have drained them to grow crops, developers have filled them to build houses, and highways have been built over others. Since vernal pools dry up for much of the year, some people do not even realize that they are there.

Vernal pools are found in many parts of the country and the world. Though many of the plants and animals found in them are different from one place to another, life in these pools is similar in many ways. In each case, life cycles of animals in the pools are tied to a seasonal rhythm of filling and drying out. Vernal pools are home to animals not found elsewhere.

More Than a Big Puddle

Vernal pools are not just big puddles in the woods. They are part of the forest. The ponds are nurseries for many forest creatures. Wood frogs live most of their lives in the forest. They are born in the pools. They spend a few months there as tadpoles. Afterward they return for only a few days each year to breed. Birds come to bathe, deer come to drink, and raccoons come to eat frogs. Most of the animals living near vernal pools use them or benefit from them. Garter snakes eat the frogs and salamanders that grow up in the pools. Flycatchers munch on adult damselflies, dragonflies, and caddisflies that emerge from the pools. The forest needs the vernal pools.

Vernal pools need the forest. The forest shades the soil and the pools. The shade keeps the sun from evaporating the water in the pools. The leaves of black gum, white oak, sweet gum, and red maple fuel these ponds. The leaves are eaten by insects and enter the food chain. The forest is the source of much of the life in the pools. Wood frogs, three kinds of treefrogs, and five kinds of salamanders come from the forest to lay their eggs in the vernal pool. The tadpoles and larvae that hatch from these eggs are an important part of the pool community. They would not survive, though, without the forest around the pool.

All across the United States and southern Canada, many vernal pools have been lost. California is rich in vernal pools. Most of the pools there are very different from our pond in Delaware, but like ours, they are important to fairy shrimp,

Vernal pools in California are full of wildflowers in spring.

salamanders, and frogs. Many kinds of wildflowers grow only in California's vernal pools. California has lost more than half of its vernal pools. Many have been replaced by agriculture or housing developments. Others have dried up because wells have sucked too much water from the ground.

Kids in Massachusetts have taken the lead in protecting vernal pools. Massachusetts has a program to register vernal pools so they can be protected more easily. To register a pool, one must map it and show photographs or other proof that vernal-pool creatures live there. Students have helped to register hundreds of vernal pools in that state. In early spring, kids have also acted as crossing guards for salamanders that must migrate across roads to reach the breeding ponds. To educate people about vernal pools, the students have created beautiful posters about the animals that live in

California vernal pools are an important part of the grasslands.

Vernal pools are great places to learn about frogs. Don't forget to put them back.

them. We can only hope that the enthusiasm of these students will spread to other states.

Taking an interest in your local vernal pool can help save it. A good way to explore vernal pools is with a dip net and a pair of waders or old tennis shoes. Be careful not to trample the plants or amphibian eggs. Put the animals in a pan of water as soon as you capture them and return them as soon as you have had a look at them. Keep a list of what you find, and draw pictures of each plant and animal you see. Once you know what lives in the pond, you can let people know how important the pond is. Make people proud of what they have, and they will not want to lose it.

Sharing what you learn about vernal pools can help save them!

Glossary

amphibians—animals with backbones that are usually born in water and breathe through gills, and later change their bodies to live on land and to breathe air. Frogs, toads, and salamanders are amphibians.

cloaca—the opening in an amphibian's body through which eggs and waste leave the body.

deciduous—describes a plant that loses its leaves for a season.

ecology—the study of the relationship between and among plants, animals, and their environment.

exoskeleton—the tough outside protective layer of the body of an insect or other arthropod.

explosive breeders—animals that breed only during a short burst of time.

food chain—a series of plants and animals in which each one eats the next.

food web—a number of food chains linked together.

metamorphose—to change from one life form or stage to another, such as from tadpole to frog.

nocturnal—active at night.

obligate species—a kind of plant or animal that is tied only to a particular environment and can live nowhere else.

pollen—tiny grains that are carried from the male part of the flower of one plant to the female part of the flower of another.

pollination—the delivery of pollen to the flower, fertilizing the female cells to produce seeds.

scavenger—an animal that eats dead animals.

spermatophore—a jelly-like package of sperm cells that is passed from the male to the female during reproduction.

terrestrial—living on land.

translucent—letting some light pass through, but not clearly.

vernal pool—a shallow seasonal pond that is wet for at least several weeks most years, has no major inlet or outlet, and usually has no fish.

Suggested Readings

Childs, Nancy, and Betsy Colburn. *Vernal Pool Lessons and Activities: A Curriculum Companion to Certified*. Lincoln, MA: Massachusetts Audubon Society, 1993.

Colburn, Betsy, and Chris Leahy. *Pond Watchers, Guide to Ponds and Vernal Pools of Eastern North America*. (Laminated sheet with illustrations and text.) Lincoln, MA: Massachusetts Audubon Society, 1995.

Colburn, Elizabeth A. *Vernal Pools: Natural History and Conservation*. Granville, OH: McDonald and Woodward Publishing, 2004.

Kenny, Leo P., and Matthew R. Burne. *A Field Guide to the Animals of Vernal Pools*. Boston: Massachusetts Division of Fisheries and Wildlife, 2000.

Wechsler, Doug. *Bullfrogs*. The Really Wild Life of Frogs series. New York: PowerKids Press, 2002.

Wechsler, Doug. *Leopard Frogs*. The Really Wild Life of Frogs series. New York: PowerKids Press, 2002.

Wechsler, Doug. *Treefrogs*. The Really Wild Life of Frogs series. New York: PowerKids Press, 2002.

Wechsler, Doug. *Wood Frogs*. The Really Wild Life of Frogs series. New York: PowerKids Press, 2002.

Web Sites

Web sites were active at time of publication.

The Vernal Pool Association. www.vernalpool.org. An informative site with detailed information about vernal pools, their inhabitants, and conservation in the Northeast.

California Vernal Pools. www.vernalpools.org. Includes many photographs and links to children's Web sites.

Index